In the Year 1945

by

Kerry Butters.

In the Year 1945

Millennium: 2nd millennium

Centuries: 19th century – **20th century** – 21st century

Decades: 1910s 1920s 1930s – **1940s** – 1950s 1960s 1970s

Years: 1942 1943 1944 – **1945** – 1946 1947 1948

1945 (MCMXLV) was a common year starting on Monday (dominical letter G) of the Gregorian calendar, the 1945th year of the Common Era (CE) and *Anno Domini* (AD) designations, the 945th year of the 2nd millennium, the 45th year of the 20th century, and the 6th year of the 1940s decade.

Contents

Events

January

January 27: The Soviet Red Army liberates Auschwitz.

- January – WWII: Allied advance from Paris to the Rhine continues; the United States Army crosses the Siegfried Line.
- January 1 – WWII:
  - Germany begins Operation Bodenplatte, an attempt by the *Luftwaffe* to cripple Allied air forces in the Low Countries.
  - The Chenogne massacre in which German prisoners were allegedly killed by American forces near the village of Chenogne, Belgium.

- January 5 – Australia recognizes the Polish Committee of National Liberation as the government of Poland.
- January 7 – WWII: British General Bernard Montgomery holds a press conference at Zonhoven describing his supporting role at the Battle of the Bulge.
- January 12 – WWII: The Soviet Union begins the Vistula–Oder Offensive in Eastern Europe against the German Army.
- January 13 – WWII: The Soviet Union begins the East Prussian Offensive to eliminate German forces in East Prussia.
- January 16 – WWII: Adolf Hitler takes residence in the *Führerbunker* in Berlin.
- January 17
  - WWII: The Soviet Union occupies Warsaw, Poland.
  - The Holocaust: A Soviet patrol arrests Raoul Wallenberg in Hungary.
- January 18 – The Holocaust: The SS begins evacuation of Auschwitz concentration camp. Nearly 60,000 prisoners, mostly Jews, are forced to march to other locations in Germany; as many as 15,000 die. The 7,000 too sick to move are left without supplies being distributed.
- January 20 – Franklin D. Roosevelt is inaugurated to a fourth term as President of the United States, the only President ever to exceed two terms.
- January 23 – WWII:
  - Hungary agrees to an armistice with the Allies.
  - German Grand Admiral Karl Dönitz orders the start of Operation Hannibal, the mass evacuation by sea of German troops and civilians from the Courland Pocket, East Prussia and the Polish Corridor.

- January 24 – WWII: AP war correspondent Joseph Morton, nine OSS men, and four SOE agents are executed by the Germans at Mauthausen concentration camp under Hitler's Commando Order of 1942 which stipulates the immediate execution of all captured Allied commandos or saboteurs without trial, even those in proper uniforms. Morton is the only Allied correspondent to be executed by the Axis during the war.
- January 26 – WWII: Infantry action at Holtzwihr, France, for which Audie Murphy is awarded the Medal of Honor.
- January 27 – The Holocaust: The Soviet Red Army liberates the Auschwitz and Birkenau concentration camps.
- January 28 – WWII: Supplies begin to reach China over the newly reopened Burma Road.
- January 30 – WWII:
  - MV *Wilhelm Gustloff*, with over 10,000 mainly civilian Germans from Gotenhafen (Gdynia) is sunk in Gdańsk Bay by three torpedoes from the Soviet submarine *S-13* in the Baltic Sea; up to 9,400 are thought to have died – the greatest loss of life in a single ship sinking in war action in history.
  - Raid at Cabanatuan: 121 American soldiers and 800 Filipino guerrillas free 813 American prisoners of war from the Japanese-held camp in the city of Cabanatuan in the Philippines.
  - Adolf Hitler makes his last public speech to be delivered personally, on broadcast radio, expressing the belief that Germany will triumph.
- January 31 – WWII: Eddie Slovik is executed by firing squad near Sainte-Marie-aux-Mines for desertion, the only

U.S. soldier since the American Civil War ever executed for this offense.

February

The "Big Three" at the Yalta Conference: Winston Churchill, Franklin D. Roosevelt and Joseph Stalin, February 2, 1945.

During the Battle of Iwo Jima, U.S. Marines land on the island, February 19, 1945.

- February
  - Anne Frank dies of typhus in the Bergen-Belsen concentration camp, Lower Saxony, Germany.
  - Raymond L. Libby of American Cyanamid's research laboratories at Stamford, Connecticut, announces a method of orally administering the antibiotic penicillin.

- ○
- February 3 – WWII:
  - ○ Battle of Manila: United States forces enter the outskirts of Manila to capture it from the Japanese Imperial Army, starting the battle.
  - ○ The Soviet Union agrees to enter the Pacific War against Japan once hostilities against Germany are concluded.
- February 4–11 – WWII: President Franklin D. Roosevelt, Prime Minister of the United Kingdom Winston Churchill and Soviet leader Joseph Stalin hold the Yalta Conference.
- February 6 – French writer Robert Brasillach is executed for collaboration with the Germans.
- February 7 – WWII: General Douglas MacArthur returns to Manila.
- February 9
  - ○ Walter Ulbricht becomes leader of the German Communists in Moscow.
  - ○ WWII: "Black Friday": A force of Allied Bristol Beaufighter aircraft suffers heavy casualties in an unsuccessful attack on German destroyer Z33 and escorting vessels sheltering in Førde Fjord, Norway.
- February 10 – WWII: 3,608 drown when the troopship SS *General von Steuben* is sunk by the Soviet submarine *S-13*.
- February 10–20 – WWII: Operation Kita: The Imperial Japanese Navy returns "Completion Force", containing both its *Ise*-class battleships, safely from Singapore to Kure in Japan despite Allied attacks.
- February 13 – WWII:

- o Soviet forces capture Budapest, Hungary, from the Nazis.
- o Royal Air Force and Unites States Army Air Forces bombing of Dresden, Germany.
- February 14 – Chile, Ecuador, Paraguay and Peru join the United Nations.
- February 16 – WWII:
  - o American and Filipino ground forces land on Corregidor Island in the Philippines.
  - o Combined American and Filipino forces recapture the Bataan Peninsula.
  - o Venezuela declares war on Germany.
- February 19–February 20 – 980 Japanese soldiers die as a result of a killing spree by long saltwater crocodiles in Ramree, Burma.
- February 19 – WWII – Battle of Iwo Jima: About 30,000 United States Marines land on Iwo Jima.
- February 21 – The last V-2-rocket is launched from Peenemünde.
- February 22 – WWII:
  - o Italian Front: end of the Battle of Monte Castello, after nearly three months of fighting, Brazilian troops expel German forces of a pivot point in the (Tuscan) North Apennines, where their artillery was impeding the advance of British 8th Army toward Bologna;
  - o Uruguay declares war on Germany and Japan.
- February 23 – WWII:
  - o Battle of Iwo Jima: A group of United States Marines reach the top of Mount Suribachi on the island and are photographed raising the American flag. The

photo, *Raising the Flag on Iwo Jima* (taken by Joe Rosenthal), later wins a Pulitzer Prize.

- The 11th Airborne Division, with Filipino guerrillas, freed the captives of the Los Baños internment camp.
- The capital of the Philippines, Manila, is liberated by combined American and Filipino ground troops.
- American and Filipino troops enter Intramuros, Manila.
- The German garrison in Poznań capitulates to Red Army and Polish troops.
- Bombing of Pforzheim: Heaviest of a series of bombing raids on Pforzheim in Germany by Allied aircraft is carried out by the British Royal Air Force. As many as 17,600 people, or 31.4% of the town's population, are killed in the raid and about 83% of the town's buildings destroyed, two-thirds of its complete area and between 80 and 100% of the inner city.
- Turkey joins the war on the allies side.

- February 24 – The Egyptian Premier Ahmad Mahir Pasha is killed in Parliament after reading a decree.
- February 28 – In Bucharest, a violent demonstration takes place, during which the *bolşevic* group opens fire on the army and protesters. In response, Andrei Y. Vishinsky, USSR vice commissioner of foreign affairs and president of the Allied Control Commission for Romania, travels to Bucharest to compel Nicolae Rădescu to resign as premier.

March

- March 1 – President Franklin D. Roosevelt gives what will be his last address to a joint session of the United States Congress, reporting on the Yalta Conference.
- March 2
  - Former U.S. Vice-President Henry A. Wallace starts his term of office as U.S. Secretary of Commerce, serving under President Franklin D. Roosevelt.
  - The rocket-propelled Bachem Ba 349 *Natter* is first test launched at Stetten am kalten Markt. The launch fails and the pilot, Lothar Sieber, dies.
- March 3 – WWII:
  - Finland declares war on the Axis powers.
  - United States and Filipino troops take Manila, Philippines.
  - Bombing of the Bezuidenhout: The British Royal Air Force accidentally bombs the Bezuidenhout neighbourhood in The Hague, Netherlands, killing 511 people.
  - A possible experimental atomic test blast occurs at the Nazis' Ohrdruf military testing area.
- March 4 – In the United Kingdom, The Princess Elizabeth, later to become Queen Elizabeth II, joins the British Army's Women's Auxiliary Territorial Service as a truck driver/mechanic.
- March 4 – Football club FC Red Star (in Serbian: *FK Crvena Zvezda*) formed in Belgrade, Yugoslavia.
- March 5 – WWII: Brazilian troops take Castelnuovo (Vergato), in the last prior operations for the Allied Spring 1945 offensive in Italy.

- March 6
  - A Communist-led government is formed in Romania under Petru Groza following Soviet intervention.
  - Resistance fighters accidentally ambush and attempt to execute SS general Hanns Albin Rauter, the arch-persecutor of the Dutch.
- March 7 – WWII: At the end of Operation Lumberjack, American troops seize the Ludendorff Bridge over the Rhine at Remagen in Germany and begin to cross; in the next 10 days 25,000 troops with equipment are able to cross.
- March 8
  - Josip Broz Tito forms a government in Yugoslavia.
  - The Nazi authorities kill 117 Dutch men in reprisal for the attempted murder of Hanns Albin Rauter.
  - Operation Sunrise: Waffen-SS General Karl Wolff meets with Allen Welsh Dulles of the United States Office of Strategic Services at Lucerne in neutral Switzerland to negotiate surrender of the Axis forces in Italy to the Allies.
- March 9–10 – WWII: Bombing of Tokyo: "Operation Meetinghouse" – USAAF B-29 bombers flying from the Mariana Islands attack Tokyo, Japan, with incendiary bombs, killing 100,000 citizens in the firebombing.
- March 9 – The film *Les Enfants du Paradis* premières in Paris.
- March 11
  - The Empire of Japan establishes the Empire of Vietnam, a puppet state which will last only until August 23, with Bảo Đại as its ruler.

- o Sammarinese general election gives San Marino the world's first democratically elected communist government, which will hold power to 1957.
- March 12 – WWII: Swinemünde is destroyed by the USAAF killing an estimated 8,000 to 23,000 civilians, mostly refugees saved by Operation Hannibal.
- March 15–31 – WWII: The Soviet Red Army carries out the Upper Silesian Offensive.
- March 15 – The 17th Academy Awards ceremony is held, broadcast via radio for the first time. Best Picture goes to *Going My Way*.
- March 16 – WWII: The Battle of Iwo Jima unofficially ends, with pockets of guerrilla resistance persisting until the official conclusion of the battle.
- March 17 – WWII: Kobe, Japan is fire-bombed by 331 B-29 bombers, killing over 8,000 people.
- March 18 – WWII: 1,250 American bombers attack Berlin.
- March 19 – WWII:
  - o Adolf Hitler orders that all industries, military installations, machine shops, transportation facilities and communications facilities in Germany be destroyed.
  - o Off the coast of Japan, bombers hit the aircraft carrier USS *Franklin*, killing about 800 of her crewmen and crippling the ship.
- March 21 – WWII:
  - o British troops liberate Mandalay, Burma.
  - o Bulgarian and Soviet troops successfully defend the north bank of the Drava River as the Battle of the Transdanubian Hills concludes.
- March 22

- Arab League is formed with the adoption of a charter in Cairo, Egypt.
- Hildesheim Cathedral in Germany is destroyed in an air raid.
- March 24
  - WWII – Operation Varsity: Two airborne divisions capture bridges across the Rhine River to aid the Allied advance.
  - The cartoon character Sylvester the cat debuts in *Life with Feathers*.
- March 26 – WWII: The Battle of Iwo Jima officially ends, with the destruction of the remaining areas of Japanese resistance.
- March 29
  - WWII: The Red Army almost destroys the German 4th Army in the Heiligenbeil Pocket in East Prussia.
  - The "Clash of Titans": George Mikan and Bob Kurland duel at Madison Square Garden in New York as Oklahoma State University defeats DePaul 52–44 in basketball.
- March 30 – WWII:
  - The Red Army pushes most of the Axis forces out of Hungary into Austria.
  - Alger Hiss is congratulated in Moscow for his part in bringing positions of Western powers and the Soviet Union closer to each other at the Yalta Conference.

April

The Japanese battleship *Yamato* explodes after persistent attacks from U.S. aircraft during the Battle of Okinawa, 7 April 1945.

Adolf Hitler, along with his wife Eva Braun, committed suicide on 30 April 1945.

- April 1 – WWII: Battle of Okinawa: The Tenth United States Army lands on Okinawa.
- April 4 – WWII:

- American troops liberate their first Nazi concentration camp, Ohrdruf extermination camp in Germany.
- The Red Army enters Bratislava and pushes to the outskirts of Vienna, taking it on April 13 after several days of intense fighting.
- April 6 – WWII:
  - Sarajevo is liberated from Nazi Germany and the Independent State of Croatia (a fascist puppet state) by Yugoslav Partisans.
  - The Battle of Slater's Knoll on Bougainville Island concludes with a decisive victory for the Australian Army's 7th Brigade.
  - Allied forces reach Merkers Salt Mines in Thuringia where gold reserves of the Nazi German Reichsbank are stored.
- April 7 – WWII:
  - The only flight of the German ramming unit known as the Sonderkommando Elbe takes place, resulting in the loss of some 24 B-17s and B-24s of the United States Eighth Air Force.
  - The Japanese battleship *Yamato* is sunk 200 miles (320 km) north of Okinawa while en route on a suicide mission.
  - Kantarō Suzuki becomes Prime Minister of Japan.
- April 8 – The SS begins to evacuate the Buchenwald concentration camp; inmates in the Buchenwald Resistance call for American aid and overpower and kill the remaining guards.
- April 9

- WWII: The Battle of Königsberg, in East Prussia, ends with Soviet forces capturing the city.
  - Abwehr conspirators Wilhelm Canaris, Hans Oster and Hans von Dohnányi are hanged at Flossenberg concentration camp, along with pastor Dietrich Bonhoeffer.
  - Johann Georg Elser, would-be assassin of Adolf Hitler, is executed at Dachau concentration camp.
- April 10 – WWII: Visoko is liberated by the 7th, 9th and 17th Krajina Brigades from the Tenth Division of Yugoslav Partisan forces.
- April 11 – Buchenwald concentration camp is liberated by the United States Army.
- April 12 – President of the United States Franklin D. Roosevelt dies suddenly at Warm Springs, Georgia; Vice President Harry S. Truman becomes the 33rd President.
  - WWII: The U.S. Ninth Army under General William H. Simpson crosses the Elbe River astride Magdeburg, and reached Tangermünde—only 50 miles from Berlin.
- April 14 – WWII: The First Canadian Army assumes military control of the Netherlands where German forces are trapped in the Atlantic wall fortifications along the coastline.
- April 15 – WWII:
  - The Bergen-Belsen concentration camp is liberated by British and Canadian forces.
  - The Canadian First Army reaches the coast in the northern Netherlands and captures Arnhem.
- April 16 – WWII:

- Battle of Berlin begins, opening with the Battle of the Oder–Neisse and the Battle of the Seelow Heights.
- Canadian forces take Harlingen, and occupy Leeuwarden and Groningen in the Netherlands.
- 6,500 drown when *Goya* is sunk by Soviet submarine L-3.

- April 17 – WWII:
  - Brazilian forces liberate the town of Montese, Italy, from German forces.
  - Inundation of the Wieringermeer in the Netherlands by occupying German forces.
- April 18 – American war correspondent Ernie Pyle is killed by Japanese machine gun fire on the island of Ie Shima off Okinawa.
- April 19 – Rodgers and Hammerstein's *Carousel*, a musical play based on Ferenc Molnár's *Liliom*, opens on Broadway and becomes their second long-running stage classic.
- April 20 – WWII: On his 56th birthday Adolf Hitler leaves his Führerbunker to decorate a group of Hitler Youth soldiers in Berlin. It will be his last trip to the surface from his underground bunker.
- April 22 – WWII:
  - Heinrich Himmler, through Count Bernadotte, puts forth an offer of German surrender to the Western Allies, but not the Soviet Union.
  - Adolf Hitler privately concedes defeat in his underground Berlin bunker after learning Felix Steiner could not mobilize enough men to launch a counterattack on the Soviets who had just broken through Germany.

- April 23 – WWII: Hermann Göring sends the Göring Telegram to Hitler seeking confirmation that he should take over leadership of Germany in accordance with the decree of 29 June 1941. Hitler regards this as treason.
- April 24 – Retreating German troops destroy all the bridges over the Adige in Verona, including the historic Ponte di Castelvecchio and Ponte Pietra.
- April 25
  - Founding negotiations for the United Nations begin in San Francisco.
  - WWII – Elbe Day: United States and Soviet troops link up at the Elbe River, cutting Germany in two.
- April 25–26 – WWII: Last major strategic bombing raid by RAF Bomber Command, the destruction of the oil refinery at Tønsberg in southern Norway by 107 Avro Lancasters.
- April 26 – WWII:
  - Battle of Bautzen: The last "successful" German panzer-offensive in Bautzen ends with the city recaptured.
  - The British 3rd Infantry Division under General Whistler captures Bremen.
  - Nazi surrenders mean the British and Canadians now control the German border with Switzerland from Basle to Lake Constance.
- April 27
  - U.S. Ordnance troops find the coffins of Frederick William I of Prussia, Frederick the Great, Paul von Hindenburg, and his wife.
  - The Western Allies flatly reject any offer of surrender by Germany other than unconditional on all fronts.
- April 28

- Benito Mussolini and his mistress, Clara Petacci, are executed by Italian partisans as they attempt to flee the country. Their bodies are then hung by their heels in the public square of Milan.
- The Canadian First Army captures Emden and Wilhelmshaven.

- April 29
  - At the royal palace in Caserta, Lieutenant-Colonel Viktor von Schweinitz (representing General Heinrich von Vietinghoff) and SS-Obersturmbannfuehrer Eugen Wenner (representing Waffen-SS General Karl Wolff) sign an unconditional instrument of surrender for all Axis powers forces in Italy, taking effect on May 2. Italian General Rodolfo Graziani orders the *Esercito Nazionale Repubblicano* forces under his command to lay down their arms.
  - Dachau concentration camp is surrendered to U.S. forces, who kill SS guards at the camp and the nearby hamlet of Webling.
  - Brazilian forces liberate the commune of Fornovo di Taro, Italy, from German forces.
  - Operation Manna: British Avro Lancaster bombers drop food into the Netherlands to prevent the starvation of the civilian population.
  - Adolf Hitler marries his longtime mistress Eva Braun in a closed civil ceremony in the Berlin Führerbunker and signs his last will and testament.
- April 30 – Death of Adolf Hitler: Adolf Hitler and his wife of one day, Eva Braun, commit suicide as the Red Army approaches the Führerbunker in Berlin. Karl Dönitz succeeds Hitler as President of Germany (*Reichspräsident*)

and Joseph Goebbels succeeds as Chancellor of Germany (*Reichskanzler*), in accordance with Hitler's political testament of the previous day.

May

May – Interpol (being headquartered in Berlin) effectively ceases to exist (it is recreated on June 3, 1946).

May 1 – WWII:

- Hamburg Radio announces that Hitler has died in battle, "fighting up to his last breath against Bolshevism."
- Joseph Goebbels and his wife Magda commit suicide after killing their six children. Karl Dönitz appoints Lutz Graf Schwerin von Krosigk as the new Chancellor of Germany in the Flensburg Government.
- Troops of the Yugoslav 4th Army, together with the Slovene 9th Corpus NOV, enter Trieste.
- Mass suicide in Demmin.

May 2 – WWII:

- The Soviet Union announces the fall of Berlin. Soviet soldiers hoist the Red flag over the *Reich Chancellery*.

- ◎

Prague liberated by Red Army in May 1945.

- Lübeck is liberated by the British Army.
- Surrender of Axis troops in Italy comes into effect.
- Troops of the New Zealand Army 2nd Division enter Trieste a day after the Yugoslavs; the German Army in Trieste surrenders to the New Zealand Army.
- Following the death or resignation of the Hitler Cabinet in Germany, the Schwerin von Krosigk cabinet first meets.
- Neuengamme concentration camp near Hamburg is evacuated at about this date.
- Expatriate American poet Ezra Pound is arrested by the Italian resistance movement; released by them, on May 5 he turns himself in to the United States Army and is imprisoned as a traitor.

May 3 – WWII:

- The prison ships *Cap Arcona*, *Thielbek* and *Deutschland* are sunk by the British Royal Air Force in Lübeck Bay.
- Rocket scientist Wernher von Braun and 120 members of his team surrender to U.S. forces (later going on to help to start the U.S. space program).
- German Protestant theologian Gerhard Kittel is arrested by the French forces in Tübingen, Germany.

May 4 – WWII:

- German surrender at Lüneburg Heath: All German armed forces in northwest Germany, Denmark and the Netherlands surrender unconditionally to Field Marshal Bernard Montgomery, officially coming into effect on May

5 at 08:00 hours British Double (and German) Summer Time.
- The Netherlands is liberated by British and Canadian troops.
- Denmark is liberated.
- Admiral Karl Dönitz orders all U-boats to cease offensive operations and return to bases in Norway.
- The Holy Crown of Hungary is found by the United States Army 86th Infantry Division. The United States government keeps the crown in Fort Knox for safekeeping from the Soviets until it is returned to Hungary on 6 January 1978.
- German auxiliary cruiser Orion is sunk on her way to Copenhagen carrying refugees; with a loss of over 3,800 lives.

May 5 – WWII:

- Prague uprising: Prague rises up against occupying Nazi forces.
- The US 11th Armored Division liberates the prisoners of Mauthausen concentration camp, including Simon Wiesenthal.

- American soldiers fighting in the Pacific theater listen to radio reports of Victory in Europe Day on May 8, 1945.
- Canadian soldiers liberate the city of Amsterdam from Nazi occupation.
- A Japanese fire balloon kills five children and a woman, Elsie Mitchell, near Bly, Oregon, when it explodes as they drag it from the woods. They are the only people killed by an enemy attack on the American mainland during WWII.
- Yosemite Sam, a cartoon character debuts in *Hare Trigger*.

- May 6
  - WWII: Mildred Gillars ("Axis Sally") delivers her last propaganda broadcast to Allied troops (the first was on December 11, 1941).
  - Holocaust: Ebensee concentration camp in Austria is liberated by troops of the 80th Division (United States).

- May 6–7 – The government of the Independent State of Croatia, the fascist puppet state established in the Croatian and Bosnian parts of occupied Yugoslavia, flees Zagreb for a location near Klagenfurt in Austria rather than fall into the hands of the Yugoslav Partisans, initiating the events of the Bleiburg repatriations.

- May 7 – WWII: General Alfred Jodl signs the unconditional German Instrument of Surrender at Reims, France, ending Germany's participation in the war, officially coming into effect on May 8 at 23:01 hours Central European Time (00:01 hours May 9 German Summer Time).
- May 8 – WWII:
  - Victory in Europe Day (V-E Day) observed by the western European powers as Nazi Germany surrenders, marking the end of WWII in Europe.
  - Shortly before midnight (May 9 Moscow time) the final German Instrument of Surrender is signed at the seat of the Soviet Military Administration in Berlin-Karlshorst, attended by representatives of the Allies.
  - Canadian troops move into Amsterdam, after German troops surrender.
  - Surrender of the Dodecanese is signed in Symi.
  - The British 8th Army, together with Slovene partisan troops and a motorized detachment of the Yugoslav 4th Army, arrives in Carinthia and Klagenfurt. The Croatian Armed Forces of the Independent State of Croatia are ordered by their commanders not to surrender to the Yugoslav Partisans but to attempt to retreat to Austria and surrender to the British, part of the events leading to the Bleiburg repatriations.
- May 8–29 – Sétif and Guelma massacre: In Algeria, thousands die as French troops and released Italian POWs kill an estimated 6,000 to 40,000 Algerian citizens.

Marines of 1st Marine Division fighting on Okinawa, May 1945.

- May 9 – WWII:
  - The Soviet Union marks V-E Day.
  - The Red Army enters Prague.
  - Hermann Göring surrenders to the United States Army near Radstadt.
  - Vidkun Quisling and other members of the collaborationist Quisling regime in Norway surrender to the Resistance (Milorg) and police at Møllergata 19 in Oslo as part of the legal purge in Norway after World War II.
  - General Alexander Löhr, Commander of German Army Group E near Topolšica, Slovenia, signs the capitulation of German occupation troops.
  - The German occupation of the Channel Islands in Guernsey and Jersey ends with their liberation by British troops.
- May 10
  - The German occupation of the Channel Islands in Sark ends with their liberation by British troops.
- May 12
  - Argentinian labour leader José Peter declares the *Meat Industry Workers Federation* dissolved.

- Rev. W. V. Awdry's children's book *The Three Railway Engines*, first of The Railway Series, is published in England.
- May 14–15 – WWII – Battle of Poljana: The last battle of the War in Europe is fought at Poljana near Slovenj Gradec, Slovenia.
- May 15 – WWII: – Bleiburg tragedy (Croatian: "Way of the Cross"): Retreating troops of the Croatian Armed Forces of the former puppet Independent State of Croatia (intermingled with fleeing civilians) attempt to surrender to the British Army at Bleiburg but are directed to surrender to Yugoslav Partisans who open fire on them. The remainder, after orders are given by Josip Broz Tito, are force-marched through Croatia and Serbia, interned or massacred, with thousands dying.
- May 16
  - The German occupation of the Channel Islands in Alderney ends with their liberation by British troops.
- May 23
  - The Flensburg Government is dissolved by the Allies and President of Germany Karl Dönitz and Chancellor of Germany Lutz Graf Schwerin von Krosigk are arrested by British forces at Flensburg. They are respectively the last German Head of state and Head of government until 1949.
  - Heinrich Himmler, former head of the Nazi SS, commits suicide in British custody.
- May 28 – William Joyce ("Lord Haw-Haw") is captured. He is later charged with high treason in London for his English-language wartime broadcasts on German radio, convicted, and then hanged in January 1946.

- May 29
  - German communists, led by Walter Ulbricht, arrive in Berlin.
  - Dutch painter Han van Meegeren is arrested for collaboration with the Nazis, but the paintings he has sold to Hermann Göring (Koch) are later found to be his own fakes.
- May 30 – The Iranian government demands that all Soviet and British troops leave the country.

June

Dwight Eisenhower and Georgy Zhukov, June 5, 1945.

- June 1 – The British take over Lebanon and Syria.
- June 5 – The Allied Control Council, military occupation governing body of Germany, formally takes power.
- June 6 – King Haakon VII of Norway returns to Norway.
- June 11
  - William Lyon Mackenzie King is re-elected as Canadian prime minister.
  - The Franck Committee recommends against a surprise nuclear bombing of Japan.
- June 12 – The Yugoslav Army leaves Trieste, leaving the New Zealand Army in control.

- June 21 – WWII: The Battle of Okinawa ends with US occupation of the island until 1972.
- June 24 – WWII: A victory parade is held in Red Square in Moscow.
- June 25 – Seán T. O'Kelly is elected the second President of Ireland.
- June 26 – The United Nations Charter is signed.
- June 29 – Czechoslovakia cedes Carpathian Ruthenia to the Soviet Union.
- June 30 – Distribution of John von Neumann's *First Draft of a Report on the EDVAC*, containing the first published description of the logical design of a computer with stored-program and instruction data stored in the same address space within the memory (von Neumann architecture).

July

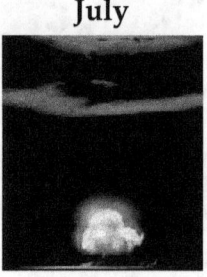

July 16: Trinity Test at night in New Mexico.

- Vannevar Bush's *As We May Think* published.
- July 1 – WWII: Germany is divided between the Allied occupation forces.
- July 5 – Australian Prime Minister John Curtin dies of a heart attack at age 60.

- July 4 – The Brazilian cruiser *Bahia* is sunk by an accidentally induced explosion, killing more than 300 and stranding the survivors in shark-infested waters.
- July 5 – WWII: The Philippines are declared liberated.
- July 8 – WWII: Harry S. Truman is informed that Japan will talk peace if it can retain the reign of the Emperor.
- July 9 – A forest fire breaks out in the Tillamook Burn (the third in that area of Oregon since 1933).
- July 15 – The Scott Morrison Award of Minor Hockey Excellence was first given; first recipient is Gordie Howe.
- July 14 – WWII: Italy declares war on Japan.
- July 16
  - The Trinity Test, the first of an atomic bomb, using about six kilograms of plutonium, succeeds in unleashing an explosion equivalent to that of 19 kilotons of TNT.
  - A train collision near Munich, Germany kills 102 war prisoners.
- July 17–August 2 – WWII: Potsdam Conference – At Potsdam, the three main Allied leaders hold their final summit of the war. President Truman officially informs Stalin that the U.S. has a powerful new weapon.
- July 21 – WWII: President Harry S. Truman approves the order for atomic bombs to be used against Japan.
- July 23 – WWII: French marshal Philippe Pétain, who headed the Vichy government during WWII, goes on trial for treason.
- July 26 – Winston Churchill resigns as Prime Minister of the United Kingdom after his Conservative Party is soundly defeated by the Labour Party in the 1945 general election. Clement Attlee becomes the new Prime Minister.

It is the first time that Labour has governed Britain with a majority in the House of Commons.

- July 26 – The Potsdam Declaration demands Japan's unconditional surrender; Article 12 permitting Japan to retain the reign of the Emperor has been deleted by President Truman.
- July 27 – WWII: Bombing of Aomori – Two USAAF B-29s dropped a total of 60,000 leaflets on the city of Aomori, Japan, warning civilians of an air raid and urge them to leave immediately.
- July 28
    - A U.S. Army Air Forces B-25 bomber crashes into the Empire State Building, killing 14 people, including all on board.
    - WWII: Japan ambiguously rejects the Potsdam Declaration.
- July 29
    - The BBC Light Programme radio station is launched, aimed at mainstream light entertainment and music.
    - WWII: Bombing of Aomori: Aomori is firebombed by 63 USAAF B-29 heavy bombers, killing 1,767 civilians and destroying 18,045 homes.
- July 30 – WWII: The heavy cruiser USS *Indianapolis* is hit and sunk by torpedoes from the Japanese submarine *I-58* in the Philippine Sea. Some 900 survivors jump into the sea and are adrift for up to four days. Nearly 600 die before help arrives. Captain Charles B. McVay III of the cruiser is later court-martialed and convicted.

August

August 9: The mushroom cloud from the nuclear bomb dropped on Nagasaki rising 18 km into the air.

September 2: Japan signs the Instrument of Surrender aboard the USS *Missouri*.

- August 6 – WWII: Atomic bombing of Hiroshima: A United States B-29 Superfortress, the Enola Gay, drops an atomic bomb, codenamed "Little Boy", on Hiroshima, Japan, at 8:15 a.m. (local time). The atomic bombings are believed to have resulted in between 129,000 and 246,000 deaths.
- August 7 – U.S. President Harry Truman announces the successful atomic bombing of Hiroshima while he is returning from the Potsdam Conference aboard the U.S.

Navy heavy cruiser USS *Augusta* (CA-31) in the middle of the Atlantic Ocean.

- August 8
    - The United Nations Charter is ratified by the United States Senate, and this nation becomes the third to join the new international organization.
    - WWII: The Soviet Union declares war on Japan.
- August 9 – WWII:
    - Atomic bombing of Nagasaki: A United States B-29 Bomber, *Bockscar*, drops an atomic bomb, codenamed "Fat Man", on Nagasaki, Japan, at 11:02 a.m. (local time).
    - Soviet–Japanese War opens: The Soviet Union begins its army offensive against Japan in the northern part of the Japanese-held Chinese region of Manchuria.
- August 10 – WWII: Japan offers to surrender to the Allies, "provided this does not prejudice the sovereignty of the Emperor".
- August 11
    - WWII: The Allies reply to the Japanese surrender offer by saying that Emperor Hirohito will be subject to the authority of the Supreme Commander of the Allied Forces.
    - The Holocaust: Kraków pogrom – Róża Berger is shot dead by Polish militia.
- August 11–25 – Soviet troops complete occupation of Sakhalin.
- August 13 – The Zionist World Congress approaches the British government to discuss the founding of the country of Israel.
-

- August 14
  - WWII: Emperor Hirohito accepts the terms of the Potsdam Declaration. His recorded announcement of this is smuggled out of the Tokyo Imperial Palace. At 19:00 hrs in Washington, D.C. (23:00 GMT), U.S. President Harry S. Truman announces the Japanese surrender.
- August 15
  - WWII: *Gyokuon-hōsō*: Emperor Hirohito's announcement of the unconditional surrender of Japan is broadcast on the radio a little after noon (12:00 Japan Standard Time is 03:00 GMT). This is probably the first time an Emperor of Japan has been heard by the common people. Delivered in formal classical Japanese and without directly referring to surrender, the recorded speech is not immediately easily understood by ordinary people. The Allies call this day Victory over Japan Day (V-J Day). This ends the period of Japanese expansionism and begins the period of Occupation of Japan. Korea gains independence.
  - The August Revolution in Vietnam begins with the Viet Minh taking over the capital Hanoi, taking advantage of the collapse of Japanese power.
  - Provisional International Civil Aviation Organization founded as a specialized agency of the United Nations.
- August 17
  - Philippines President José P. Laurel issues an Executive Proclamation putting an end to the Second

Philippine Republic, thus ending to his term as President of the Philippines.

- ○ Proclamation of Indonesian Independence: Indonesian nationalists Sukarno and Mohammad Hatta declare the independence of the Republic of Indonesia, with Sukarno as president and Mohammad Hatta as vice-president, igniting the Indonesian National Revolution against the Dutch Empire.
- ○ The allegorical dystopian novella *Animal Farm* by George Orwell, a satire on Stalinism, is first published by Fredric Warburg in London.
- August 19 – Chinese Civil War: Mao Zedong and Chiang Kai-shek meet in Chongqing to discuss an end to hostilities between the Communists and the Nationalists.
- August 23 – Soviet–Japanese War – Joseph Stalin orders the detention of Japanese prisoners of war in the Soviet Union.
- August 30 – WWII: Vietnam's capital Hanoi is overthrown by the Viet Minh which ends the French occupation in what becomes North Vietnam and thus the southern provinces become South Vietnam. This ends the August Revolution.
- August 31
  - ○ WWII: Allied troops arrest German field marshal Walther von Brauchitsch.
  - ○ A team at American Cyanamid's Lederle Laboratories, Pearl River, New York, led by Yellapragada Subbarow, announces they have obtained folic acid in a pure crystalline form. This

vitamin is abundant in green leaf vegetables, liver, kidney, and yeast.

September

- September 2 – WWII ends:
  - Japanese general Tomoyuki Yamashita surrenders to Filipino and American forces at Kiangan, Ifugao.
  - The final official Japanese Instrument of Surrender is accepted by the Supreme Allied Commander, General Douglas MacArthur, and Fleet Admiral Chester W. Nimitz for the United States, and delegates from the United Kingdom, Australia, New Zealand, the Netherlands, China, and others from a Japanese delegation led by Mamoru Shigemitsu, on board the American battleship USS *Missouri* in Tokyo Bay.
  - General Douglas MacArthur is given the title of Supreme Commander Allied Powers, and is also tasked with the occupation of Japan.
- September 2 – Democratic Republic of Viet Nam is officially established, by Ho Chi Minh.
- September 3 – The earliest events of the Cold War begin.
- September 4 – WWII: Japanese forces surrender on Wake Island after hearing word of their country's surrender.
- September 5
  - Iva Toguri D'Aquino, a Japanese American suspected of being wartime radio propagandist "Tokyo Rose", is arrested in Yokohama.
  - The Russian code clerk Igor Gouzenko comes forward with numerous documents implicating the

Soviet Union in many spy rings in North America: both in the United States and in Canada.

- September 8
  - American troops occupy southern Korea, while the Soviet Union occupies the north, with the dividing line being the 38th parallel of latitude. This arrangement proves to be the indirect beginning of a divided Korea which will lead to the Korean War in 1950.
- September 9 – Chiang Kai-shek officially accepts the Japanese capitulation at Nanking.
- September 10 – Vidkun Quisling is sentenced to death as a Nazi collaborator, in Norway.
- September 11
  - Hideki Tōjō, Japanese prime minister during most of WWII, attempts suicide to avoid facing a war crimes tribunal.
  - *Radio Republik Indonesia* starts broadcasting.
  - The Batu Lintang camp in Sarawak, Borneo is liberated by Australian forces.
- September 12 – The Japanese Army formally surrenders to the British in Singapore.
- September 18 – Typhoon Makurazaki in Japan kills 3,746 people.
- September 20 – Mohandas Gandhi and Jawaharlal Nehru demand that all British troops depart India.

October

October 24: The United Nations is formed. This was its flag.
The modern version is slightly retouched.

October 18: Nuremberg trials begin, after Buchenwald closed.

- October – Arthur C. Clarke puts forward the idea of a geosynchronous communications satellite in a *Wireless World* magazine article.
- October 1–15 – Operation Backfire: Three A4 rockets are launched near Cuxhaven in order to show Allied forces the rocket with liquid fuel.
- October 2– George Albert Smith becomes president of The Church of Jesus Christ of Latter-day Saints.
- October 4 – The Partizan Belgrade sports club is founded in Belgrade, Serbia.
- October 5 – Hollywood Black Friday: A strike by the Set Decorator's Union in Hollywood results in a riot.

- October 8–15 – Hadamar Trial: Personnel of the Hadamar Euthanasia Centre, now in the American zone of Allied-occupied Germany, are the first to be tried for systematic extermination in Nazi Germany.
- October 9 – Pierre Laval is sentenced to death for collaboration with the Nazis in Vichy France.
- October 14 – Czechoslovakia: A new provisional national assembly is elected.
- October 15 – WWII: Pierre Laval, the former premier of Vichy France, is shot dead by a firing squad for treason against France.
- October 15–21 – The Fifth Pan-African Congress is held in Manchester.
- October 16 – Food and Agriculture Organization established at a meeting in Quebec City as a specialized agency of the United Nations.
- October 17 – A massive number of people, headed for the General Confederation of Labour (Argentina), gather in the Plaza de Mayo in Buenos Aires to demand Juan Perón's release. This is known to the Peronists as the *Día de la lealtad* (Loyalty Day) and considered the founding day of Peronism.
- October 18 – Isaías Medina Angarita, president of Venezuela, is overthrown by a military coup.
- October 19 – Members of the Indonesian People's Army attack Anglo-Dutch forces in Indonesia.
- October 20 – Mongolians vote for independence from China.
- October 21 – Women's suffrage: Women are allowed to vote in the French Legislative Election for the first time.

- October 22 – Rómulo Betancourt is named provisional president of Venezuela.
- October 23 – Jackie Robinson signs a contract with the Montreal Royals baseball team.
- October 24
  - The United Nations is founded by ratification of its Charter, by 29 nations.
  - The International Court of Justice ("World Court") established by the United Nations Charter.
  - The Norwegian Nazi leader Vidkun Quisling is shot dead by a firing squad for treason against Norway.
- October 25 – Getúlio Vargas is deposed as president in Brazil. José Linhares is named as temporary president.
- October 27–November 20 – Indonesian National Revolution: Battle of Surabaya – Pro-independence Indonesian soldiers and militia fight British and British Indian troops in Surabaya.
- October 29
  - Getúlio Vargas resigns as the president of Brazil.
  - At Gimbels Department Store in New York City, the first ballpoint pens go on sale at $12.50 each.
- October 30 – The undivided country of India joins the United Nations.

November

- Astrid Lindgren's children's book *Pippi Långstrump* is published in Sweden and its English translation as *Pippi Longstocking* is also issued.
- November 1
  - International Labour Organization's new constitution comes into effect.

- o John H. Johnson publishes the first issue of the magazine *Ebony*.
- o Telechron introduces the model 8H59 Musalarm, the first clock radio.
- November 5 – Colombia joins the United Nations.
- November 6 – Indonesians reject an offer of autonomy from the Dutch.
- November 9 – Soo Bahk Do Moo Duk Kwan is founded.
- November 11 – Marshal Josip Broz Tito and the People's Front win a deciding majority (85%) in the Yugoslavian assembly.
- November 15
  - o Harry S. Truman, Clement Attlee, and Mackenzie King share nuclear information with the U.N. and call for a United Nations Atomic Energy Commission.
  - o An offensive is begun in Manchuria by the Chinese Nationalists against further infiltration by the Chinese Communists.
- November 16
  - o Charles de Gaulle is unanimously elected president of France by the provisional government.
  - o Cold War: The United States controversially imports 88 German scientists to help in the production of rocket technology.
  - o Agreement for the foundation of UNESCO (United Nations Educational, Scientific and Cultural Organization) at a meeting in London.
  - o *Casper the Friendly Ghost, an animated character debuts in The Friendly Ghost.*

- The motion picture *The Lost Weekend*, starring Ray Milland, is released. The most realistic film portrayal of alcoholism up to this time, it wins several Academy Awards in the following year.
- Yeshiva College is founded in New York City.
- November 18 – The Tudeh party starts a bloodless coup and will form Azerbaijan within days. Soviet troops prevent Iranian troops from getting involved.
- November 20 – The Nuremberg trials begin: Trials against 22 Nazi war criminals of WWII start at the Nuremberg Palace of Justice.
- November 26 – U.S. Ambassador to China Patrick J. Hurley resigns after he is unable to broker a deal between Chiang Kai-shek and Mao Tse Tung.
- November 28 – An earthquake in Balochistan causes a tsunami and kills 4,000.
- November 29
  - The Socialist Federal Republic of Yugoslavia is declared (this day is celebrated as Republic Day until the 1990s). Marshal Tito is named president.
  - Assembly of the world's first general purpose electronic computer, the Electronic Numerical Integrator Analyzer and Computer (ENIAC), is completed in the United States, covering 1,800 square feet (170 m^2) of floor space, and the first set of calculations is run on it.

December

- December 2
  - General Eurico Gaspar Dutra is elected president of Brazil.

- o French banks (Banque de France, BNCI, CNEP, Crédit Lyonnais, and Société Générale) nationalized.
- December 3 – Communist demonstrations in Athens presage the Greek Civil War.
- December 4 – By a vote of 65–7, the United States Senate approves the entry of the United States into the United Nations.
- December 5 – A flight of United States Navy Grumman TBF Avenger torpedo bombers known as Flight 19 disappears on a training exercise from Naval Air Station Fort Lauderdale.
- December 21 – General George S. Patton dies from injuries sustained in a car accident on December 9 in Germany.
- December 27
  - o Twenty-eight nations sign an agreement creating the World Bank.
  - o Terror strikes are carried out against British military bases in Palestine.

Date unknown

- A team at Oak Ridge National Laboratory led by Charles Coryell discovers chemical element 61, the only one still missing between 1 and 96 on the periodic table, which they will name promethium. Found by analysis of fission products of irradiated uranium fuel, its discovery is not made public until 1947.
- The first geothermal milk pasteurization is done in Klamath Falls, Oregon.

Births

January

Rod Stewart

Tom Selleck

- January 3 – Stephen Stills, American rock singer and songwriter
- January 4 – Richard R. Schrock, American chemist, Nobel Prize laureate
- January 7 – Shulamith Firestone, Canadian American feminist and writer (d. 2012)
- January 10
  - Gunther von Hagens, Polish Anatomist and inventor
  - Jennifer Moss, British actress (d. 2006)
  - Steven P. Perskie, American politician and judge
  - Rod Stewart, British rock singer
- January 11 – Christine Kaufmann, German actress

- January 12 – André Bicaba, Burkinabé sprinter
- January 14 – Einar Hákonarson, Icelandic painter
- January 15
  - Vince Foster, American deputy White House counsel during the first term of President Bill Clinton (d. 1993)
  - Princess Michael of Kent, German-born member of the British Royal Family
- January 20 – Robert Olen Butler, American writer
- January 25 – Leigh Taylor-Young, American actress
- January 26 – Jacqueline du Pré, English cellist (d. 1987)
- January 27 – Harold Cardinal, Cree political leader, writer, and lawyer (d. 2005)
- January 28
  - Karen Lynn Gorney, American actress
  - Chuck Pyle, American country-folk singer-songwriter (d. 2015)
- January 29
  - Jim Nicholson, Northern Irish politician
  - Tom Selleck, American actor
- January 30 – Michael Dorris, American author (d. 1997)
- January 31 – Joseph Kosuth, American artist

February

Bob Marley

Mia Farrow

Hans-Adam II of Liechtenstein

Brenda Fricker

- February 3
  - Roy 'Chubby' Brown, British stand-up comedian
  - Bob Griese, American football player
  - Philip Waruinge, Kenyan boxer
- February 5 – Sarah Weddington, American attorney
- February 6 – Bob Marley, Jamaican reggae singer, songwriter and musician (d. 1981)

- February 7 – Gerald Davies, Welsh rugby player
- February 9 – Mia Farrow, American actress
- February 12
  - Maud Adams, Swedish actress
  - David D. Friedman, American economist
- February 13 – Simon Schama, English Historian
- February 14 – Prince Hans-Adam II of Liechtenstein
- February 15 – Douglas Hofstadter, American cognitive scientist
- February 16 – Jeremy Bulloch, English actor
- February 17 – Brenda Fricker, Irish actress
- February 20 – Henry Polic II, American actor (d. 2013)
- February 24 – Barry Bostwick, American actor
- February 25
  - Elkie Brooks, English singer
  - Roy Saari, American swimmer (d. 2008)
- February 26 – Marta Kristen, Norwegian actress
- February 27 – Carl Anderson, American singer and actor (d. 2004)
- February 28 – Bubba Smith, American football player and actor (d. 2011)

March

Eric Clapton

George Miller

- March 1 – Dirk Benedict, American actor
- March 3
  - George Miller, Australian film director
  - Hattie Winston, American actress
- March 4
  - Dieter Meier, Swiss singer and children's writer
  - Tommy Svensson, Swedish football manager and player
  - Gary Williams, American basketball coach
- March 7
  - John Heard, American actor
  - Arthur Lee, American musician (d. 2006)
- March 8
  - Jim Chapman, American politician
  - Micky Dolenz, American actor, director and rock musician (The Monkees)
  - Anselm Kiefer, German painter
- March 9
  - Katja Ebstein, German singer
  - Dennis Rader, American serial killer
- March 13 – Anatoly Fomenko, Russian mathematician
- March 15 – A. K. Faezul Huq, Bangladeshi lawyer and politician (d. 2007)
- March 17 – Katri Helena, Finnish singer

- March 20
  - Jay Ingram, Canadian television host, author and journalist
  - Bobby Jameson, American singer-songwriter (d. 2015)
  - Pat Riley, American basketball coach
- March 26
  - Mikhail Voronin, Russian gymnast (d. 2004)
- March 28 – Rodrigo Duterte, 16th President of the Philippines
- March 29
  - Walt Frazier, American basketball player
  - Willem Ruis, Dutch game show host (d. 1986)
- March 30 – Eric Clapton, English rock guitarist
- March 31 – Gabe Kaplan, American actor, comedian, and professional poker player

April

Björn Ulvaeus

- April 2
  - Jürgen Drews, German singer
  - Linda Hunt, American actress
- April 4 – Daniel Cohn-Bendit, French activist
- April 5 – Cem Karaca, Turkish musician (d. 2004)
- April 7 – Werner Schroeter, German film director (d. 2010)

- April 9 – Peter Gammons, American baseball sportswriter
- April 11 – Christian Quadflieg, German actor
- April 12 – Lee Jong-wook, Korean Director-General of the World Health Organization (d. 2006)
- April 13
  - Tony Dow, American actor, producer, and director (*Leave It to Beaver*)
  - Lowell George, American rock musician (Little Feat) (d. 1979)
  - Bob Kalsu, American football player (d. 1970)
- April 14
  - Ritchie Blackmore, English rock guitarist (Deep Purple)
  - Tuilaepa Aiono Sailele Malielegaoi, Prime Minister of Samoa
- April 24 – Doug Clifford, American drummer
- April 25
  - Stu Cook, American bassist (Creedence Clearwater Revival)
  - Björn Ulvaeus, Swedish rock songwriter (ABBA)
- April 27 – August Wilson, American playwright (d. 2005)
- April 29
  - Hugh Hopper, British musician (d. 2009)
  - Tammi Terrell, American soul singer (d. 1970)

May

Laurent Gbagbo

Priscilla Presley

- May 1 – Rita Coolidge, American pop singer
- May 4 – Narasimhan Ram, Indian journalist
- May 5 – Kurt Loder, American film critic, author, and television personality
- May 6
    - Jimmie Dale Gilmore, American musician
    - Bob Seger, American rock singer
- May 8 – Keith Jarrett, American musician
- May 9 – Jupp Heynckes, German football manager and former footballer
- May 14 – Yochanan Vollach, Israeli footballer and president of Maccabi Haifa, CEO
- May 15 – Duarte Pio, Duke of Braganza, heir to the Portuguese crown
- May 16 – Nicky Chinn, English rock songwriter (Sweet, Suzi Quatro)
- May 17 – Tony Roche, Australian tennis player
- May 19 – Pete Townshend, English rock guitarist and lyricist (The Who)
- May 21
    - Richard Hatch, American actor

- o Ernst Messerschmid, German physicist and astronaut
- May 22 – Victoria Wyndham, American actress (*Another World*)
- May 23
  - o Lauren Chapin, American child actress and evangelist
  - o Doris Mae Oulton, Canadian community developer
- May 24 – Priscilla Presley, American actress and businesswoman
- May 28 – John Fogerty, American rock singer (Creedence Clearwater Revival)
- May 29 – Gary Brooker, English pianist and singer (Procol Harum)
- May 30 – Gladys Horton, American singer (The Marvelettes) (d. 2011)
- May 31
  - o Rainer Werner Fassbinder, German film director (d. 1982)
  - o Laurent Gbagbo, President of Côte d'Ivoire

June

Wolfgang Schüssel

Aung San Suu Kyi

Radovan Karadžić

- June 1 – Frederica von Stade, American mezzo-soprano
- June 2 – Jon Peters, American film producer
- June 3 – Hale Irwin, American professional golfer
- June 4
  - Anthony Braxton, American composer and musical instrumentalist
  - Gordon Waller, Scottish singer-songwriter and guitarist (d. 2009)
- June 5
  - John Carlos, American athlete
  - Théophile Georges Kassab, Catholic prelate (d. 2013)
  - Don Reid, American singer (The Statler Brothers)
- June 6 – David Dukes, American actor (d. 2000)
- June 7
  - Billy Butler, American singer-songwriter (d. 2015)
  - Wolfgang Schüssel, Chancellor of Austria

- June 8 – Steven Fromholz, American singer-songwriter (d. 2014)
- June 9 – Nike Wagner, German woman of the theater
- June 10 – Benny Gallagher, Scottish singer-songwriter and multi-instrumentalist, half of the duo Gallagher and Lyle
- June 11 – Adrienne Barbeau, American actress, television personality and author
- June 12 – Pat Jennings, Northern Irish footballer player
- June 13 – Rodney P. Rempt, American admiral
- June 14 – Jörg Immendorff, German painter
- June 15 – Françoise Chandernagor, French writer
- June 16
  - Claire Alexander, Canadian ice hockey player
  - Ivan Lins, Latin Grammy-winning Brazilian musician
- June 17
  - P. D. T. Acharya, Secretary General Lok Sabha
  - Frank Ashmore, American actor
  - Art Bell, American radio talk show host
  - Ken Livingstone, British politician
  - Eddy Merckx, Belgian cyclist
- June 19
  - Radovan Karadžić, Serbian politician
  - Aung San Suu Kyi, Myanmar poet, politician, recipient of the Nobel Peace Prize
  - Greil Marcus, American music journalist and cultural critic
- June 20 – Anne Murray, Canadian singer
- June 24 – George Pataki, Governor of New York
- June 25 – Carly Simon, American singer-songwriter

- June 26 – Dwight York, American musician, fashion consultant, cult leader, and child molester
- June 27 – Lu Sheng-yen, leader of the True Buddha School
- June 28 – David Knights, British bassist (Procol Harum)
- June 29 – Chandrika Kumaratunga, President of Sri Lanka

July

Debbie Harry

Helen Mirren

- July 1 – Debbie Harry, American rock singer (Blondie)
- July 6 – Burt Ward, American actor
- July 7
  - Michael Ancram, British politician
  - Matti Salminen, Finnish bass singer
- July 8 – Micheline Calmy-Rey, Swiss Federal Councilor
- July 9 – Dean Koontz, American writer
- July 10 – Ron Glass, American actor

- July 11 – Richard Wesley, American playwright and screenwriter
- July 15 – Jürgen Möllemann, German politician (d. 2003)
- July 16 – Victor Sloan, Irish artist
- July 17 – Alexander, Crown Prince of Yugoslavia
- July 18 – Boomer Castleman, American singer-songwriter (d. 2015)
- July 20
  - Kim Carnes, American singer-songwriter
  - Larry Craig, U.S. politician
  - John Lodge, English rock singer and songwriter (The Moody Blues)
- July 21 – John Lowe, English darts player
- July 24 – Azim Premji, Indian businessman
- July 26 – Dame Helen Mirren, British actress
- July 28 – Jim Davis, American cartoonist
- July 30
  - Roger Dobkowitz, American game show producer
  - Patrick Modiano, French novelist, Nobel Prize laureate

August

Steve Martin

Vince McMahon

Van Morrison

- August 1 – Douglas D. Osheroff, American physicist, Nobel Prize laureate
- August 2 – Joanna Cassidy, American actress
- August 4 – Alan Mulally, American businessman, former CEO of the Ford Motor Company
- August 5
  - Loni Anderson, American actress
  - Ja'net Dubois, American actress and singer
- August 6 – Ron Jones, British director (d. 1993)
- August 7 – Alan Page, American football player
- August 9 – Posy Simmonds, English cartoonist
- August 13 – Howard Marks, Welsh drug smuggler and author (d. 2016)
- August 14
  - Steve Martin, American actor and comedian
  - Eliana Pittman, Brazilian singer and actress

- o Wim Wenders, German film director and producer
- August 19 – Ian Gillan, English rock singer (Deep Purple)
- August 20 – Jonathan Goodson, American television game show producer and son of Mark Goodson
- August 22 – Ron Dante, American rock singer, songwriter, and record producer (The Archies)
- August 24 – Vincent K. "Vince" McMahon, American professional wrestling promoter, chairman and CEO of WWE
- August 25 – Daniel Hulet, Belgian cartoonist (d. 2011)
- August 26 – Tom Ridge, American politician
- August 27 – Marianne Sägebrecht, German film actress
- August 31
    - o Van Morrison, Irish rock musician
    - o Itzhak Perlman, Israeli-American violinist and conductor

September

Franz Beckenbauer

Ehud Olmert

- September 1 – Mustafa Balel, Turkish writer
- September 4 – Danny Gatton, American guitarist (d. 1994)
- September 5 – Al Stewart, Scottish singer-songwriter
- September 7 – Jacques Lemaire, Canadian ice hockey coach
- September 8
  - Kelly Groucutt, British Bassist (Electric Light Orchestra) (d. 2009)
  - Ron "Pigpen" McKernan, American musician (Grateful Dead) (d. 1973)
  - Rogatien Vachon, Canadian ice hockey player
- September 9 – Doug Ingle, American songwriter and singer for Iron Butterfly
- September 10 – José Feliciano, Puerto Rican singer
- September 11 – Franz Beckenbauer, German footballer and coach
- September 12 – Richard Thaler, American economist
- September 14 – Martin Tyler, British sports broadcaster
- September 15 – Jessye Norman, American soprano
- September 16 – Pat Stevens, American voice actress (d. 2010)
- September 17 – Phil Jackson, American basketball coach
- September 19 – Randolph Mantooth, American actor and motivational speaker
- September 20
  - Candy Spelling, American socialite and writer
  - Laurie Spiegel, American electronic composer
- September 21
  - Shaw Clifton, General of the Salvation Army
  - Kay Ryan, American poet

- September 23 – Paul Petersen, child actor and advocate of other child actors
- September 25 – Dee Dee Warwick, American singer (d. 2008)
- September 26 – Bryan Ferry, English singer-songwriter and musician (Roxy Music)
- September 27 – Jack Goldstein, Canadian artist (d. 2003)
- September 29 – Nadezhda Chizhova, Russian athlete
- September 30 – Ehud Olmert, 12th Prime Minister of Israel

October

John Lithgow

Luiz Inácio Lula da Silva

- October 1 – Donny Hathaway, American soul singer-songwriter (d. 1979)
- October 2 – Don McLean, American rock singer-songwriter

- October 3
  - Kay Baxter, American bodybuilder (d. 1988)
  - Viktor Saneyev, Soviet athlete
- October 4 – Clifton Davis, American actor
- October 5 – Brian Connolly, Scottish musician (d. 1997)
- October 6 – Ivan Graziani, Italian singer-songwriter (d. 1997)
- October 12
  - Aurore Clément, French actress
  - Dusty Rhodes, American wrestler (d. 2015)
- October 13 – Susan Stafford, American television presenter
- October 15 – Jim Palmer, American baseball player
- October 18
  - Huell Howser, American television personality, host of *California's Gold* (d. 2013)
  - Norio Wakamoto, Japanese voice actor
  - Yıldo, Turkish showman, footballer
- October 19
  - Angus Deaton, Scottish-born economist, recipient of the Nobel Memorial Prize in Economic Sciences
  - John Lithgow, American actor
- October 20 – George Wyner, American actor
- October 22 – Yvan Ponton, Canadian actor and sportscaster
- October 23 – Kim Larsen, Danish rock musician.
- October 24 – Eugenie Scott, Executive Director of the National Center for Science Education
- October 25
  - Peter Ledger, Australian artist (d. 1994)
  - David Schramm, American astrophysicist (d. 1997)

- October 26 – Pat Conroy, American author (d. 2016)
- October 27
  - Luiz Inácio Lula da Silva, 35th President of Brazil
  - Carrie Snodgress, American actress (d. 2004)
- October 29 – Melba Moore, American singer and actress
- October 29 – Daniel Albright, American literary critic and musicologist
- October 30 – Henry Winkler, American actor, producer and director
- October 31 – Brian Doyle-Murray, American actor

November

Neil Young

Goldie Hawn

James Avery

- November 3 – Gerd Müller, German footballer
- November 5 – Jacques Lanctôt, Canadian terrorist
- November 7
  - Bob Englehart, American editorial cartoonist
  - Waljinah, Javanese singer
- November 12
  - Michael Bishop, American author
  - Tracy Kidder, American journalist and author
  - Neil Young, Canadian singer-songwriter and musician
- November 15 – Anni-Frid Lyngstad, Norwegian rock singer (ABBA)
- November 18
  - Wilma Mankiller, Chief of the Cherokee Nation (d. 2010)
  - Mahinda Rajapaksa, President of Sri Lanka
- November 21 – Goldie Hawn, American actress
- November 23 – Jerry Harris, American sculptor
- November 24 – Nuruddin Farah, Somali novelist
- November 26
  - Daniel Davis, American actor
  - John McVie, English rock musician (Fleetwood Mac)
- November 27
  - Barbara Anderson, American actress
  - James Avery, American actor (d. 2013)

- November 30 – Mary Millington, British porn star (d. 1979)

December

Bette Midler

Lemmy

- December 1 – Bette Midler, American actress, comedian and singer
- December 2 – Charles "Tex" Watson, American prisoner
- December 7 – Clive Russell, English actor
- December 9 – Michael Nouri, American actor
- December 12 – Portia Simpson-Miller, Prime Minister of Jamaica
- December 13 – Kathy Garver, American actress, author and online radio hostess
- December 16 – Patti Deutsch, American voice actress
- December 17

- o Ernie Hudson, American actor
- o Chris Matthews, American news anchor
- December 19 – Elaine Joyce, American actress and game show panelist
- December 20
  - o Peter Criss, American rock drummer (KISS)
  - o Sivakant Tiwari, senior legal officer of the Singapore Legal Service (d. 2010)
- December 22 – Diane Sawyer, American news journalist
- December 24
  - o Lemmy, English rock singer and bassist (Motörhead) (d. 2015)
  - o Nicholas Meyer, American screenwriter, producer, director and novelist
- December 25 – Gary Sandy, American actor (*WKRP in Cincinnati*)
- December 26 – John Walsh, American media personality
- December 28 – Birendra of Nepal (d. 2001)
- December 30 – Davy Jones, English-born pop singer and actor (*The Monkees*) (d. 2012)
- December 31
  - o Barbara Carrera, Nicaraguan-born American actress
  - o Vernon Wells, Australian film and television actor

Deaths

January

Else Lasker-Schüler

- January 2 – Bertram Ramsay, British admiral (b. 1883)
- January 3 – Edgar Cayce, American mysticist (b. 1877)
- January 6
  - Josefa Llanes Escoda, Filipino advocate of women's suffrage and founder of the Girl Scouts of the Philippines (b. 1898)
  - Herbert Lumsden, British general (killed in action) (b. 1897)
  - Vladimir Vernadsky, Soviet mineralogist and geochemist (b. 1863)
- January 7 – Thomas McGuire, American World War II fighter ace (b. 1920)
- January 9
  - Dennis O'Neill, Welsh child killed by his foster parents, which scandal resulted in an overhaul of the British Care Systems (b. 1932)
  - Jüri Uluots, Estonian statesman (b. 1890)
- January 19
  - Petar Bojović, Serbian field marshal (b. 1858)

- Gustave Mesny, French Army general (b. 1886)
- January 21 – Archibald Murray, British Army general (b. 1860)
- January 22 – Else Lasker-Schüler, German poet and author (b. 1869)
- January 23 – Newton E. Mason, United States Navy rear admiral (b. 1850)
- January 30
  - William Goodenough, British admiral (b. 1867)
  - Pedro Paulet, Peruvian scientist (b. 1874)
- January 31 – Eddie Slovik, American soldier (executed) (b. 1920)

February

Anne Frank

- Anne Frank, German-born Jewish diarist and writer (typhus in Bergen-Belsen concentration camp) (b. 1929)
- February 1
  - Prince Kiril of Bulgaria (b. 1895)
  - Bogdan Filov, 28th Prime Minister of Bulgaria (executed) (b. 1883)
- February 2
  - Adolf Brand, German writer (b. 1874)

- o Joe Hunt, American tennis champion (b. 1919)
- February 3 – Roland Freisler, Nazi German judge (b. 1893)
- February 5
  - o Denise Bloch, French World War II heroine (b. 1915)
  - o Lilian Rolfe, French World War II heroine (b. 1914)
  - o Violette Szabo, French/British World War II heroine (b. 1921)
- February 6 – Robert Brasillach, French writer (executed) (b. 1909)
- February 10 – Anacleto Díaz, Filipino jurist (murdered during the Battle of Manila) (b. 1878)
- February 11 – Al Dubin, Swiss songwriter (b. 1891)
- February 12 – Antonio Villa-Real, Filipino jurist (murdered during the Battle of Manila) (b. 1878)
- February 15 – Helmut Möckel, German youth leader and politician (b. 1909)
- February 17 – Gabrielle Weidner, Belgian World War II heroine (b. 1914)
- February 21 – Eric Liddell, Scottish runner (b. 1902)
- February 25 – Mário de Andrade, Brazilian writer and photographer (b. 1893)
- February 26
  - o James Roy Andersen, American general (b. 1904)
  - o Millard Harmon, American general (b. 1888)

March

David Lloyd George

Hans Fischer

Takeichi Nishi

Tadamichi Kuribayashi

- March 2 – Emily Carr, Canadian artist (b. 1871)
- March 3 – Aleksandra Samusenko, Soviet WWII tank commander (b. 1922)
- March 4
  - Lucille La Verne, American actress (b. 1872)

- ○ Mark Sandrich, American director (b. 1900)
- March 5
  - ○ Albert Richards, British war artist (b. 1919)
  - ○ Rupert Downes, Australian general (b. 1885)
  - ○ George Vasey, Australian general (b. 1895)
- March 8 – Frederick Bligh Bond, English architect (b. 1864)
- March 12 – Friedrich Fromm, German Nazi official (executed) (b. 1888)
- March 16 – Börries von Münchhausen, German poet (b. 1874)
- March 18 – William Grover-Williams, French race car driver and war hero (b. 1903)
- March 20 – Lord Alfred Douglas, English poet (b. 1870)
- March 22
  - ○ Enrico Caviglia, Italian marshal (b. 1862)
  - ○ Eliyahu Bet-Zuri, Israeli assassin (executed) (b. 1922)
  - ○ Eliyahu Hakim, Israeli assassin (executed) (b. 1925)
  - ○ John Hessin Clarke, American Supreme Court Justice (b. 1857)
  - ○ Takeichi Nishi, Japanese gold medalist at the 1932 Summer Olympics and tank commander at Iwo Jima (b. 1902)
- March 23 – Élisabeth de Rothschild, French WWII heroine (b. 1902)
- March 26
  - ○ David Lloyd George, Welsh former Prime Minister of the United Kingdom and Liberal politician (b. 1863)
  - ○ Tadamichi Kuribayashi, Imperial Japanese Army general and commander of the battle of Iwo Jima (probably killed in action) (b. 1891)

- o Boris Shaposhnikov, Soviet military leader, Marshal of the Soviet Union (b. 1882)
- March 27 – Halid Ziya Uşaklıgil, Turkish author (b. 1867)
- March 29 – Ferenc Csik, Hungarian swimmer (b. 1913)
- March 30
    - o Élise Rivet, French nun and war heroine (b. 1890)
    - o Maurice Rose, American general (killed in action) (b. 1899)
- March 31
    - o Harriet Boyd Hawes, American archaeologist (b. 1871)
    - o Hans Fischer, German chemist, Nobel Prize laureate (b. 1881)
    - o Torgny Segerstedt, Swedish newspaper editor and publicist (b. 1876)

April

Franklin D. Roosevelt

Benito Mussolini

Adolf Hitler

- April – Auguste van Pels, German-Jewish housemate of Anne Frank (b. 1900) (exact date unknown)
- April 5 – Huldreich Georg Früh, Swiss composer (b. 1903)
- April 7
  - Elizabeth Bibesco, British writer (b. 1897)
  - Seiichi Itō, Japanese admiral (killed in action) (b. 1890)
- April 9
  - Dietrich Bonhoeffer, German theologian (hanged) (b. 1906)
  - Wilhelm Canaris, head of the German Abwehr (hanged) (b. 1887)
- April 10
  - Gloria Dickson, American actress (b. 1917)
  - H.N. Werkman, Dutch artist and printer (b. 1882)
  - Walther Wever, German fighter ace (killed in action) (b. 1923)
- April 12 – Franklin D. Roosevelt, 32nd President of the United States (b. 1882)
- April 13 – Ernst Cassirer, German philosopher (b. 1874)
- April 18

- Arthur Andrew Cipriani, Trinidad and Tobago labour leader (b. 1875)
- Ernie Pyle, American journalist (killed in action) (b. 1900)
- William, Prince of Albania (b. 1876)
- April 21 – Walter Model, German field marshal (suicide) (b. 1891)
- April 22 – Käthe Kollwitz, German artist (b. 1867)
- April 24 – Ernst-Robert Grawitz, German Reichsphysician (S.S. and Police) in the Third Reich (probable suicide) (b. 1899)
- April 28
  - Hermann Fegelein, German Nazi general (executed) (b. 1906)
  - Benito Mussolini, Italian Duce of Fascism (executed) (b. 1883)
  - Clara Petacci, mistress of Benito Mussolini (executed) (b. 1912)
  - Nicola Bombacci, Italian Fascist politician (executed) (b. 1879)
  - Achille Starace, Italian Fascist politician (executed) (b. 1889)
  - Alessandro Pavolini, Italian Fascist politician (executed) (b. 1903)
  - Roberto Farinacci, Italian Fascist politician (executed) (b. 1892)
- April 29 – Malcolm McGregor, American actor (b. 1892)
- April 30
  - William Darby, American creator of the U.S. Army Rangers (b. 1911)
  - Luisa Ferida, Italian actress (b. 1914)

- Adolf Hitler, German Nazi Führer and Chancellor (suicide) (b. 1889)
- Eva Braun, wife of Adolf Hitler (suicide) (b. 1912)

May

Joseph Goebbels

Heinrich Himmler

- May 1
  - Joseph Goebbels, German Nazi propaganda minister (suicide) (b. 1897)
  - Magda Goebbels, wife of Joseph Goebbels (suicide) (b. 1901)
- May 2 – Martin Bormann, German Nazi leader (probable suicide) (b. 1900)
- May 4 – Fedor von Bock, German field marshal (killed in action) (b. 1880)
- May 5 – Peter van Pels, German-Jewish love interest of diarist Anne Frank (b. 1926)

- May 8
  - Ernst-Günther Baade, German general (died of wounds) (b. 1897)
  - Wilhelm Rediess, SS and Police Leader of Nazi-occupied Norway (suicide) (b. 1900)
  - Josef Terboven, *Reichskommissar* of Nazi-occupied Norway (suicide) (b. 1898)
  - Bernhard Rust, education minister of Nazi Germany (suicide) (b. 1883)
- May 10 – Konrad Henlein, Sudeten German Nazi leader (suicide) (b. 1898)
- May 11 – Kiyoshi Ogawa, Japanese kamikaze pilot (killed in action) (b. 1922)
- May 14 – Heber J. Grant, 7th president of The Church of Jesus Christ of Latter-day Saints (b. 1856)
- May 15 – Charles Williams, British author (b. 1886)
- May 16 – Kaju Sugiura, Japanese admiral (killed in action) (b. 1896)
- May 17 – Bobby Hutchins, American Our Gang films child actor (b. 1925)
- May 18 – William Joseph Simmons, American founder of the second Ku Klux Klan (b. 1880)
- May 19 – Philipp Bouhler, German Nazi leader (suicide) (b. 1899)
- May 23 – Heinrich Himmler, German head of the SS (suicide) (b. 1900)
- May 24 – Robert Ritter von Greim, German field marshal (suicide) (b. 1892)
- May 31 – Odilo Globocnik, Austrian Nazi leader (suicide) (b. 1904)

June

- June 4 – Georg Kaiser, German dramatist (b. 1878)
- June 7 – Kitaro Nishida, Japanese philosopher (b. 1870)
- June 8 – Robert Desnos, French poet and resistance fighter (b. 1900)
- June 13 – Minoru Ōta, Japanese admiral (suicide) (b. 1891)
- June 15 – Nikola Avramov, Bulgarian painter (b. 1897)
- June 16
  - Henry Bellamann, American writer (b. 1882)
  - Nikolai Berzarin, Soviet Red Army general (b. 1904)
  - Aris Velouchiotis, Greek World War II resistance leader (b. 1905)
- June 18 – Simon Bolivar Buckner, Jr., American general, killed in action at Okinawa (b. 1886)
- June 22
  - Isamu Chō, Japanese general (suicide) (b. 1895)
  - Mitsuru Ushijima, Japanese general (suicide) (b. 1887)
- June 23 – Giuseppina Tuissi, Italian resistance member (b. 1923)
- June 24 – José Gutiérrez Solana, Spanish painter (b. 1886)
- June 27 – Emil Hácha, 3rd President of Czechoslovakia and State President of Protectorate of Bohemia and Moravia (b. 1872)

July

- July 2 – Óscar Benavides, 67th and 76th President of Peru (b. 1876)
- July 5 – John Curtin, 14th Prime Minister of Australia (b. 1885)

- July 12 – Wolfram Freiherr von Richthofen, German field marshal (b. 1895)
- July 13 – Alla Nazimova, Russian actress (b. 1879)
- July 16 – Addison Randall, American actor (b. 1906)
- July 17 – Ernst Busch, German field marshal (b. 1885)
- July 20 – Paul Valéry, French poet (b. 1871)
- July 28 – Margot Asquith, Countess of Oxford and Asquith (b. 1864)
- July 31 – Artemio Ricarte, Filipino general (b. 1866)

August

Robert H. Goddard

- August 2 – Pietro Mascagni, Italian composer (b. 1863)
- August 9
  - Harry Hillman, American athlete (b. 1881)
  - Tosaka Jun, Japanese philosopher (b. 1900)
- August 10 – Robert Goddard, American rocket scientist (b. 1882)
- August 15
  - Korechika Anami, Japanese general (b. 1887)
  - Matome Ugaki, Japanese admiral (b. 1890)
- August 16 – Takijirō Ōnishi, Japanese admiral (b. 1891)
- August 18 – Subhas Chandra Bose, Indian political leader (b. 1897)

- August 19 – Tomás Burgos, Chilean philanthropist (b.1875)
- August 25 – Willis Augustus Lee, American admiral (b. 1888)
- August 29 – Fritz Pfleumer, German engineer and inventor (b. 1881)
- August 26 – Franz Werfel, Austrian writer (b. 1890)
- August 31 – Stefan Banach, Polish mathematician (b. 1892)

September

Johannes Hans Geiger

Béla Bartók

- September 1 – Frank Craven, American actor (b. 1881)
- September 6 – John S. McCain, Sr., American admiral (b. 1884)
- September 12 – Sugiyama Hajime, Japanese general (b. 1880)
- September 15 – Anton Webern, Austrian composer (b. 1883)

- September 16 – John McCormack, Irish tenor (b. 1884)
- September 20
  - Jack Thayer, American survivor of the sinking of the RMS *Titanic* (b. 1894)
  - Eduard Wirths, German doctor, chief SS doctor at Auschwitz concentration camp (suicide) (b. 1909)
  - Augusto Tasso Fragoso, Brazilian soldier and statesman (b. 1969)
- September 24 – Hans Geiger, German physicist and inventor (b. 1882)
- September 26
  - Béla Bartók, Hungarian composer (b. 1881)
  - A. Peter Dewey, first American casualty in Vietnam (b. 1916)
  - Kiyoshi Miki, Japanese philosopher (b. 1897)

October

Pierre Laval

- October 10 – Joseph Darnand, Vichy France politician (executed) (b. 1897)
- October 13 – Milton S. Hershey, American chocolate tycoon (b. 1857)
- October 15 – Pierre Laval, Prime Minister of France (executed) (b. 1883)
- October 19

- ○ Plutarco Elías Calles, President of Mexico (b. 1877)
- ○ N. C. Wyeth, American illustrator (b. 1882)
- October 21 – Henry Armetta, Italian actor (b. 1888)
- October 24 – Vidkun Quisling, Norwegian traitor (executed) (b. 1887)
- October 25 – Robert Ley, German Nazi politician (suicide) (b. 1890)
- October 26 – Paul Pelliot, French explorer (b. 1878)
- October 28 – Gilbert Emery, American actor (b. 1875)
- October 31
  - ○ Ignacio Zuloaga, Basque Spanish painter (b. 1870)
  - ○ Henry Ainley, English actor (b. 1879)

November

- November 7 – Gus Edwards, American songwriter (b. 1879)
- November 8 – August von Mackensen, German field marshal (b. 1849)
- November 11 – Jerome Kern, American composer (b. 1885)
- November 16 – Sigurður Eggerz, Prime Minister of Iceland during World War I (b. 1875)
- November 20 – Francis William Aston, English chemist, Nobel Prize laureate (b. 1877)
- November 21
  - ○ Robert Benchley, American humorist, theater critic, and actor (b. 1889)
  - ○ Ellen Glasgow, American novelist (b. 1873)
  - ○ Alexander Patch, United States Army lieutenant general, World War II army commander (b. 1889)

- November 23 – Charles Armijo Woodruff, 11th Governor of American Samoa (b. 1884)
- November 25 – Doris Keane, American stage actress (b. 1881)
- November 27 – Josep Maria Sert, Spanish Catalan muralist (b. 1874)
- November 28 – Dwight F. Davis, American tennis player (b. 1879)

December

George S. Patton

- December 1 – Anton Dostler, German general (executed) (b. 1891)
- December 4 – Thomas Hunt Morgan, American biologist, geneticist and embryologist, Nobel Prize in Physiology (b. 1866)
- December 5 – Cosmo Lang, Archbishop of Canterbury (b. 1864)
- December 13
    - Juana Bormann, Nazi concentration camp guard (executed) (b. 1893)
    - Henri Dentz, French general (b. 1881)
    - Irma Grese, warden at Bergen-Belsen concentration camp (executed) (b. 1923)

- o Josef Kramer, commandant of Bergen-Belsen concentration camp (executed) (b. 1906)
  - o Elisabeth Volkenrath, supervisor at Nazi concentration camps (executed) (b. 1919)
- December 14 – Forrester Harvey, Irish actor (b. 1884)
- December 16 – Fumimaro Konoe, Prime Minister of Japan (b. 1891)
- December 19 – Leonard F. Wing, American general and Vermont politician (b. 1893)
- December 21 – George S. Patton, American general (b. 1885)
- December 22 – Otto Neurath, Austrian philosopher and political economist (b. 1892)
- December 25 – Duy Tân, emperor of Vietnam (b. 1899)
- December 26
  - o Russell Gleason, American actor (b. 1907)
  - o Roger Keyes, 1st Baron Keyes, British admiral (b. 1872)
- December 28 – Theodore Dreiser, American author (b. 1871)

Nobel Prizes

- Physics – Wolfgang Pauli
- Chemistry – Artturi Ilmari Virtanen
- Physiology or Medicine – Sir Alexander Fleming, Ernst Boris Chain, Sir Howard Walter Florey
- Literature – Gabriela Mistral
- Peace – Cordell Hull

In the News

Adolf Hitler moves into his underground bunker, the so-called Fuhrerbunker.

US Troops Liberate Buchenwald, Germany Concentration Camp.

Dachau concentration camp liberated.

President Roosevelt, British Prime Minister Winston Churchill and Soviet leader Josef Stalin sign the Yalta Agreement.

The first German war crimes trial begins in Nuremberg.

The capital of Burma, Mandalay, is liberated by British Troops.

Italian partisans execute Benito Mussolini.

British troops liberate Belsen Concentration camp finding no running water and thousands of dead and rotting corpses.

The first atomic bombs are dropped on Hiroshima and Nagasaki in Japan in an attempt to end the Second World War.

Emperor Hirohito announces Japan's surrender on the radio.

V-E Day (Victory in Europe, as Nazi Germany surrenders) commemorates the end of World War II in Europe.

Adolf Hitler and his wife of one day, Eva Braun, commit suicide.

Joseph Goebbels and his wife commit suicide after killing their 6 children.

The United States celebrate V-J Day (Victory in Japan).

U.S. President Franklin D. Roosevelt is inaugurated for his fourth term in office in January.

Franklin Delano Roosevelt (1933-1945) dies in office; Vice President Harry S. Truman (1945-1953) takes the Oath of Office.

U.S. Navy Flight 19 disappears over the Bermuda triangle.

A US Bomber Crashes into the 79th Floor of The Empire State Building.

www.ingramcontent.com/pod-product-compliance
Lightning Source LLC
Chambersburg PA
CBHW071223280526
45787CB00002B/788